Francisco Franco: The Life and Legacy of the Controversial Spanish Dictator

By Charles River Editors

About Charles River Editors

Charles River Editors provides superior editing and original writing services across the digital publishing industry, with the expertise to create digital content for publishers across a vast range of subject matter. In addition to providing original digital content for third party publishers, we also republish civilization's greatest literary works, bringing them to new generations of readers via ebooks.

Sign up here to receive updates about free books as we publish them, and visit Our Kindle Author Page to browse today's free promotions and our most recently published Kindle titles.

Introduction

Francisco Franco

"We do not believe in government through the voting booth. The Spanish national will was never freely expressed through the ballot box. Spain has no foolish dreams." – Francisco Franco

The Spanish Civil War has exerted a powerful impact on the historical imagination. Without question, the conflict was a key moment in the 20th century, a precursor to World War II, and an encapsulation of the rise of extremist movements in the 1930s, but it was also a complex narrative in and of itself, even as it offered a truly international theatre of war. It marked one of the seminal moments, along with the 1929 Wall Street Crash, between the two apocalyptic wars of the early 20th century, and since it occurred between 1936 and 1939, Spain proved to be a testing ground of tactics, weaponry, and ideology ahead of World War II. For the Allied powers Britain and France, Spain became a nadir of "appeasement," yet, as the name suggests, the conflict had distinctly Spanish characteristics. The pressures that led to war were particular to the country, its social challenges, and its long and intricate history, and it was a conflict between two sides that included disparate elements like the clergy, socialists, landowners, and even anarchists. It is estimated that somewhere between 500,000-2,000,000 people were killed in the war.

Unlike World War II, the Spanish conflict attracted artists and writers, many of whom reflected upon events and even volunteered to fight. Pablo Picasso's painting *Guernica*, journalist Martha Gellhorn's reports, Robert Capa's iconic photography, George Orwell's *Homage to Catalonia*, and Ernest Hemingway's *For Whom the Bell Tolls* are just some examples of the art and literature that documented the war, and 80 years later, the conflict and its causes still inspire musicians and writers.

Ultimately, the forces of reaction, led by General Francisco Franco, triumphed, and after his victory in 1939, Franco ruled Spain with an iron fist for 36 years. Thus, it's only natural that Franco's rapid yet unlikely rise to power in Spain came to define a country for several generations. Franco was influenced by the wider trends and forces of the 20th century, yet he would indelibly make his mark on Spain in his own right, and in the process become one of the most widely derided figures in contemporary history.

Born in the last decade of the 19th century, Franco was nevertheless synonymous with a number of trends of the 20th. In particular, his life was intertwined with the extremist ideologies of the era, in particular fascism and communism, and later the Cold War between the West and the communist bloc. In essence, however, Franco was a military man. He joined the army as a teenager and made his name as an officer in Spain's wars in Africa. When the country cast off its monarchy and declared a Republic in 1931, Franco – although relatively restrained politically during the period – stood for order and maintaining the army's role in Spanish society. When a group of officers launched a rebellion in July 1936, Franco quickly joined the army's uprising and rapidly rose to the top of the nationalist's chain of command.

After his victory in the Spanish Civil War, Franco used political ideas and ideology as it suited him, though he did seem to advocate conservatism, militarism, Catholicism and monarchism. Franco adeptly steered Spain through the Second World War and the Cold War without really committing the country to any specific engagements, but he still managed to secure support and backing from more powerful allies.

For the people of Spain, however, Franco was far from the benevolent figurehead he portrayed himself to be. Franco's rule was vicious and spiteful, and persecution and oppression were ever present during his dictatorship. Franco's Spain was intolerant of dissent, and by the 1970s, the country appeared to outsiders to be completely under his control and influence. It seemed likely that his successors would continue to rule in his image or, more worryingly, that far left groups would challenge a post-Franco autocrat.

What actually happened in Spain after Franco seemed one of the least likely outcomes. When he died in November 1975, Franco looked to have completely triumphed in his life's objectives. Spain was utterly molded into his image: conservative, strongly religious and relatively stable. Opposition to his rule, particularly of the kind that had he fought against during the civil war, was quieted. Franco had appointed a successor, the young monarch Juan Carlos, who the

Caudillo was sure would continue down the road that he had pursued for almost 40 years. Yet, in the end, Franco failed spectacularly, and within three years of his death a new constitution had been enacted that put in place a democracy and enshrined liberal and progressive values. Meanwhile, Spain's regions, another issue detested by Franco, such as Catalonia and the Basque Country, secured significant autonomy within the new constitution. The conservative model installed by Franco, which lacked women's rights, linguistic recognition, or trade unions, was overturned. In short, the country that seemed so durable under Franco was completely changed within the space of a few tumultuous years, demonstrating that Franco's legacy proved remarkably fragile and vulnerable.

Nevertheless, his life – controversial as it was – holds huge significance both for Spain and Europe. *Francisco Franco: The Life and Legacy of the Controversial Spanish Dictator* examines one of the 20th century's most notorious leaders, and how he affected Spain and Europe. Along with pictures of important people, places, and events, you will learn about Franco like never before.

Franco's Early Life

Francisco and his parents

Francisco Franco was born in Ferrol, Galicia, in northern Spain, on December 4, 1892 into a religious and conservative family. His parents, the 37-year-old Nicolás Franco y Salgado Araújo and María del Pilar Bahamonde y Pardo de Andrade, ten years younger, were relatively affluent. Franco had four siblings, two sisters and two brothers although his sister María de la Paz did not live into adulthood. The men in Franco's family tended to join the Spanish navy and this was also to be expected of the young Francisco.

Ferrol, located in the A Coruña province of Galicia, is in the north-west tip of Spain. Facing the Atlantic coast, it was unsurprising that the young Francisco aspired to join the navy. Six generations of the Franco family had served in the Spanish navy and it was assumed that this would continue.[1] His family was completely integrated into a naval, middle class way of life. As a teenager Francisco sought to join up and, like his father and ancestors, obtain a commission

---

[1] George Hills, *Franco: The Man and His Nation* (London: Robert Hale, 1967), pp. 15-33.

and eventually serve as an officer.

As a youth Francisco was brought up in a stifling atmosphere. It has been written that Franco's family was isolated and also personally remote and cold and that Franco carried these traits with him into adulthood.[2] The world in which he came of age, however, was changing. The Spanish Naval Academy accepted no new recruits between 1906 and 1913. This was the setting in which a young Franco was denied access into the Spanish navy and ultimately forced, or so his family believed, to enroll with the army.

Franco and his brother Nicolás

For hundreds of years Spain had been one of the world's great powers. It dominated the high seas and had a substantial empire, particularly in Central and South America. Nevertheless, the country had been in decline for some time by the start of the 20th century. The core of Spain's relative decline was its inability to keep up with its contemporaries during the 18th and 19th centuries. Britain and France, as well as the Netherlands and latterly Germany, had all

---

[2] Ibid, p. 20.

industrialized and taken on a market economy. To varying extents, other European powers had also implemented liberalizing political reforms, emboldening entrepreneurs, stimulating innovation and heading off social unrest. Spain, on the other hand, was still overwhelmingly rural, had only partially industrialized and was by no means a capitalist economy, let alone politically liberal. A short lived Spanish Republic existed in 1873-74 but was soon overthrown by the military. In fact, military coups had become somewhat endemic in Spain, therefore making the consolidation of democracy particularly difficult.

It was this environment in which Franco was brought up. For conservative Spaniards, like his own family, the apparent decline of the country was a tragedy. Spain had lost most of its colonies in the early 19th century, as part of the independence movements that gripped Latin America, initiated by Simón Bolívar and others. At the end of the century, Spain lost its territories in Cuba and the Philippines, humiliated by the rising power of the United States. Spain had been laid low by its inability to keep up with its contemporaries and the poor performance of its armed forces. It was the latter trend that conservatives in Spain focused on. Many also believed that the country was in moral decline and sought to consolidate the position of the Catholic Church in Spanish society. These themes animated Franco throughout his long life.

Eager to enlist into the military but blocked from naval college, Franco disappointed his navy father by joining the army in 1907, aged just 14. The elder Franco, Nicolas, has been described as a "bad-tempered authoritarian," and young Francisco, unable to win his father's "acceptance and affection," became more introverted and lonely.[3] Nevertheless, Franco embraced life as an army cadet. He graduated from the Infantry Academy in 1910 and was given a commission and posted to Spanish Morocco in 1912 as a young officer. It was the start of a decorated military career that would culminate in the country's highest rank.

At the time Spain was fighting the so-called Rif War, which lasted intermittently from 1909-1926. The Rif region is a mountainous, tribal area near to the northwestern tip of today's Morocco, including Tangiers and Ceuta, and opposite the Spanish mainland. Europeans had long attempted to settle and dominate the region, and Spain pushed into the area in 1909. Historians have claimed that the Rif War was more about the Spanish military attempting to regain some of the competence which had been clearly lost in its defeats at the hands of the Americans in Cuba and the Philippines. The incursions stimulated a local insurgency against the Spanish, and later the French, that ensured the conflict dragged on for almost two decades. Casualties probably totaled reached the tens of thousands on both sides, but for Franco, it was an opportunity to show his mettle.

Franco was said to have been a courageous soldier and certainly received plaudits from his superiors for his performance in Morocco. He was shot in the stomach and injured at El Biutz in 1916, and after his recovery, Franco progressed rapidly through the ranks. He was promoted to

---

[3] Paul Preston, *Franco: A Biography* (London: HarperCollins, 1993), p. 3.

second in command in the Spanish Foreign Legion, which was founded in 1920 and was directly modeled on its French counterpart. The efficacy of the Foreign Legion was deemed crucial to the eventual Spanish victory and included several nationalities, most significantly Moroccans themselves. This regiment was dubbed the "Army of Africa" and developed a fearsome reputation within Spain. It would eventually be most remembered for its role in the Spanish Civil War.

On October 22, 1923 Franco married María del Carmen Polo y Martínez-Valdès, better known as Carmen Polo. The couple had one child, daughter María del Carmen, who was born in 1926.

Vicente Martin's picture of Franco and his wife

Political Fragility

The same year Franco married Carmen Polo, Spain was convulsed by another coup, this one led by Miguel Primo de Rivera, who acted in concert with King Alfonso XIII and the military. A general in the Spanish army who had fought in Spanish Morocco and the Rif region, Primo de Rivera took power from the parliamentary government.

Miguel Primo de Rivera

King Alfonso XIII

At the time, the war in Africa was not going well. The 1921 Battle of Annual (approximately 85 kilometers from the Spanish enclave of Melilla) was a major defeat for the Spanish army and became known as the "Disaster" in Spain. As news of the defeat filtered back to the mainland, people soured on the government, which only lasted a matter of months before falling to the next crisis. There was also plenty of social unrest. Socialist (UGT, *Unión General de Trabajadores* or the General Union of Workers) and anarchist (CNT, *Confederación Nacional del Trabajo* or National Work Confederation) unions attempted to stage a general strike across the country although ultimately the protests subsided. A general strike had previously been crushed by the army in 1917. The anarchist movement had a unique history in Spain and was particularly strong in Catalonia. Socialism, on the other hand, was strong throughout Europe and beyond. These movements were potent in Spain, where poverty was still widespread, and presented an existential threat to the status quo. This trend would recur over the following decade and would prove to be another key reason Franco came to power.

The country had also experienced economic problems in the wake of the First World War even though it had not been a combatant. The military was concerned that the civilian administration wanted to abolish the monarchy and reduce the power of the army.

As Prime Minister between 1923 and 1930, Primo de Rivera ruled as a military dictator. Franco had not been involved in the 1923 coup, and accounts suggest that he and his contemporaries were not particularly sympathetic to Primo de Rivera.[4] However, Franco was probably not opposed to military rule in principle,[5] and under Primo de Rivera, Franco progressed further up the ranks. Insurgents in the Rif declared a Republic in 1921, independent of both Spain and Morocco, so Spanish forces attempted to extinguish the breakaway region. In 1925, Franco, now a colonel, launched an amphibious landing at Al Hoceima. The ensuing campaign finally brought an end to the Rif conflict and Franco's role was given wide commendation. King Alfonso XIII requested a meeting with the young officer and promoted Franco to Brigadier General in February 1926. He was the youngest general in the Spanish Army at the age of 33.

Two years later, Franco was appointed head of the Army training academy in Zaragoza, in Aragon, and he would be the head of the Military Academy for three years, until 1931. This role proved invaluable in his later role as military leader of the nationalists in the Spanish Civil War, particularly when he was one of the army officers who rebelled in 1936. It is estimated that 95% of his former army cadets at the Zaragoza academy supported Franco in 1936, thereby siding with the nationalist forces. Franco had already shown that he could inspire intense loyalty amongst his subordinates.

The Republic

By the late 1920s, Spain had already experienced 50 years of intermittent instability, and it would now enter a more acute phase. The immediate cause for upheaval was economic turbulence elsewhere, as the October 1929 Wall Street Crash in the United States reverberated around the world, particularly in Europe. Many European countries had experienced growth in the 1920s, but the fundamentals of several economies, especially after the devastation of the First World War, were weak.

Although Spain was not as severely affected as other European countries – most notably Germany – the negative impact nevertheless caused significant problems. The country was essentially a developing and industrializing economy. Only a number of cities were comparable to contemporary European industrial centers, such as Barcelona, Madrid, Bilbao, and Valencia. Much of the country was poor and peasants still toiled on land owned by wealthier aristocrats and the ruling class. Spain therefore needed economic growth to help satisfy the economic and

---

[4] Paul Preston, *Franco: A Biography* (London: HarperCollins, 1993), p. 40.
[5] Ibid, p. 41.

social needs of its population. Unfortunately, General Primo de Rivera ruled the country in an economically uneven fashion during the 1920s.

Primo de Rivera governed Spain as a relatively orthodox military autocrat. He believed he was reluctantly fulfilling a temporary role to restore morality to Spanish society and to enhance the country's standing and reputation. The coup, after all, had happened as a result of the military disasters in Morocco. Franco certainly took important lessons from Primo de Rivera's time in office, both from his errors, even as he sympathized with Primo de Rivera's broad aims and objectives. Primo de Rivera suspended the 1876 constitution, the so-called Restoration, and enacted a number of measures that would later be replicated by Franco. These included press censorship, suppressing regional aspirations (like in Catalonia), and banning the CNT union. The Catalan flag, anthem, and some customs such as traditional dancing were prohibited.

Primo de Rivera managed to conclude the Rif War within three years and could claim some kind of victory. The general also attempted to consolidate and increase the role of the Catholic Church in Spanish society, for instance by deepening the link between education and religion.[6]

Primo de Rivera could possibly point to some achievements, most notably presiding over seven years of relative stability, but they were all bought at the cost of widespread repression. His supervision of the economy was incompetent, and he eventually managed to alienate his core supporters, the Spanish aristocracy. As unemployment rose at the end of the decade, Primo de Rivera set out a plan of public works to provide jobs and economic growth. The plan was relatively traditional, but he planned to pay for it through loans and increasing taxes on the wealthy. As well as infuriating the rich, and their allies in the military, Primo's economic policies caused inflation. His policies – conservative authoritarianism combined with a centrally planned economy including infrastructure and public works – had a proto-fascist flavor, and indeed his son, José Antonio, was to develop the model more vigorously.

In January 1930, General Primo de Rivera stepped down after the military made it clear they no longer fully supported him. The general fled to France and died less than two months later of complications linked to diabetes. Spain was about to enter a new crisis and Franco would soon be thrust into the spotlight.

King Alfonso XIII had strongly supported Primo de Rivera, and as a result, his own reputation became tightly aligned with the military leader. After Primo stepped down, Alfonso appointed another general, Dámaso Berenguer, as head of the government. As with so much of 20th century Spain, however, it was the military and the landed gentry that made the key decisions. Primo de Rivera had estranged these key groups with his economic policies, and they now tied that to the king. Social unrest again stirred in Catalonia and Spain was still suffering the effects

[6] 'M. Primo de Rivera: Coup and Success', *Spain: Then and Now*, http://www.spainthenandnow.com/spanish-history/m-primo-de-rivera-coup-and-success, [accessed 19 June 2018]

of the global depression.

In April 1931, the king fled Spain after General José Sanjurjo informed him he had lost the confidence of the military. Soon afterwards the Second Spanish Republic was proclaimed and the monarchy was abolished.

When the Spanish Republic was announced in 1931, Franco was still head of the Military Academy in Zaragoza. He was not necessarily opposed to the new arrangement, given that the military had played a key role in bringing down the monarchy and the dictatorship of Primo de Rivera, but the Republic quickly moved in a direction that unsettled Franco and his allies in the military. Elections were held soon after the proclamation of the Republic in 1931, and a coalition of liberals and progressives formed a government.

For many Spaniards this presented a period of great hope. The new administration offered land reform, increased access to education, improved rights for women, greater autonomy for Spain's regions, and a reduced role for the Catholic Church and the military. Some of these changes were implemented quickly – such as regional autonomy – but others, most notably land reform, were met by heavy resistance from vested interests. In these respects, Franco was adept at keeping a low profile during the Republic years. Military reform, however, almost immediately enraged the young general and led many in Spain to speculate that the Republic's aim was to "triturar el Ejército" ("crush the army").[7]

On June 3, 1931, the Republican Minister for War, Manuel Azaña, opened a review of promotions in the military, including a retroactive inquiry into the Moroccan wars.[8] This potentially meant a number of high-ranking military figures may have been demoted. The move outraged figures like Francisco Franco, and the inquiry took 18 months to complete, antagonizing the almost 1,000 officers effected. Meanwhile, on June 30, Azaña closed the Military Academy in Zaragoza, putting Franco out of a job. Azaña believed the training facility was too expensive and that the academy was a potential "hotbed" of right-wing reactionary militarism, a belief that proved quite prescient.[9] As the eminent historian on 20th century Spain, Paul Preston, noted, "This guaranteed Azaña the eternal enmity of its Director, General Franco."[10]

---

[7] Paul Preston, *The Spanish Civil War: Reaction, Revolution & Revenge* (London: Harper Perennial, 2006), p. 48.
[8] Ibid, p. 47.
[9] Ibid, p. 48.
[10] Ibid, p. 48.

Azaña

The Second Spanish Republic existed from 1931-1936 and progressed in three distinct phases, with one center-left government, one right-wing government and the final chaotic months before civil war broke out. Franco only turned against the Republic, at least openly, in the final days before a military coup began in July 1936.

The first phase, between 1931-1933, was the most optimistic for Spain and, in the final analysis, the most moderate. Nevertheless, a number of issues quickly arose that concerned the conservatives in Spain, and its adherents like Franco. The Republican government was attempting to reduce the influence of the military in political affairs and furthermore sought to break up the large land estates and roll back the role of the church. The last point became most acute for conservative and religious Spaniards, of which there were many. Republican leaders such as Azaña appeared unconcerned when churches were attacked and priests and nuns even killed. This was perhaps the issue that truly fired up popular support for the subsequent right-wing rebellion.[11]

During this time, Franco was secretive and enigmatic.[12] Although outwardly not politically

[11] George Hills, *Franco: The Man and His Nation* (London: Robert Hale, 1967), p. 173.
[12] Francisco J. Romero Salvado, *20th-Century Spain: Politics and Society in Spain, 1898-1998* (Basingstoke:

active, he subscribed to the *Acción Española* journal, which represented monarchist opinion as well as conspiracy theories involving Jews, Freemasons (of whom Franco was a particularly rabid critic),[13] and Bolsheviks. There is evidence that demonstrates that Franco did indeed believe in some of these absurdities. The narrative, however, had a dual purpose for right-wingers during this period: to rally support against the Republican government and as propaganda.[14] Franco and other conservatives in the higher echelons of Spanish society were keen to promulgate conspiracy theories about an alleged communist takeover.[15] In this way, those on the right managed to convince the Spanish middle class that their cause was necessary and therefore dampened dissent when the coup eventually came. These beliefs would also align easily with the fascist movements that were forming all over Europe. A more general fear from conservatives such as Franco was that socialism (and anarchism) and its variants posed a threat to "Christian Europe."

The Republican leadership clearly distrusted the army, an institution that had launched numerous coups in Spain recently, and though it is not clear Franco was singled out for special treatment, he was nonetheless without a posting for six months in 1931 before being assigned a role in the Balearic Islands. General Sanjurjo launched an attempted military takeover in 1932 that failed and led to his imprisonment. Franco was not involved and even wrote to Sanjurjo admonishing his actions.

Macmillan, 1999), p. 104.
[13] Paul Preston, *Franco: A Biography* (London: HarperCollins, 1993), p. 700.
[14] Ibid, p. 330.
[15] Herbert R. Southworth, *Conspiracy and the Spanish Civil War: The Brainwashing of Francisco Franco*, (Routledge, 2002), p. 191.

Sanjurjo

The Republic, however, was a fragile entity. The government had disappointed many with the supposed timidity of its land reforms and animated conservatives by the threat it posed to the status quo. Over the five years of its existence, the ability of the Republic to bring together Spain's various factions was deemed ineffective by a growing proportion of society. Between 1931 and 1936, more and more Spaniards lost faith in the power of democracy, and eventually Franco became one of them.

In 1934, however, general elections were held, bringing a right-wing coalition into government, and with that, General Franco was rehabilitated within the Republic. A series of fragile right-wing administrations held power between elections in 1934 and 1936 (the last in the Second Republic). Franco was given greater clout under the right-wing governments, but he is best – or most infamously – known during this period for his role in the Asturias uprising. In October 1934, anarchists and socialists attempted a general strike across the country, and although it was relatively easily contained in most areas, the Asturias region proved more intractable. Situated on the Atlantic coast, the strategically important Asturias mines gave the strikers more influence and simultaneously made the government more determined to bring the recalcitrant protestors under control.

The Minister of War, Diego Hidalgo, passed on responsibility for quelling the strikes to General Franco. There was sound logic to this because Franco had previously served in the region, had participated in the army's actions against the 1917 strikers, and also knew Asturias through his wife Carmen Polo, who was from Oviedo, in the region.[16] Franco apparently viewed the strikers much like he viewed his opponents in the Moroccan conflict. In this way he could use the same, brutal tactics to fight a "frontier war."[17] As a result, Franco deployed the "Army of Africa" from his days in the Spanish Legion, and breating the uprising in a comparable fashion to the Rif War, Franco's forces crushed the strikers in Asturias. It is estimated that 1,000-2,000 strikers were killed by the army, through heavy artillery attacks as well as bombing from the air.[18] In addition, atrocities against women and children were committed by Franco's soldiers. This pattern would be repeated on a much larger scale in the civil war.

For his part, Franco told a journalist that his forces were targeting "socialism, communism and whatever attacks civilization in order to replace it with barbarism."[19] To objective watchers, Franco's crushing of the Asturias miners was disproportionate, vicious, and ruthlessly embellished. Conservative, wealthy and even middle-class Spaniards, however, supported the actions, and since they were terrified of a revolutionary takeover of the country, Franco had positioned himself as a defender of the status quo. He would be able to build on this when civil war erupted, but even by the start of it, his potential supporters were already in place.

The action in Asturias is considered by some historians as the real beginning of the Spanish Civil War, and it was certainly an event that further polarized society. Violence was always present within Republican Spain, but Asturias took this to a new level, and Franco had clearly positioned himself on the conservative side of the argument. In the aftermath, Hidalgo essentially made Franco his personal advisor on military matters, and this first real taste of politics[20] appeared to hold appeal for the general, who was then promoted by new Minister of War Gil-Robles to Chief of the General Staff in 1935.[21]

The right-wing government, however, collapsed in February 1936 and elections were called. The left had lost out in 1934 because of widespread divisions, and leftist politicians were determined not to repeat the same mistake in February 1936. Left-leaning Republicans such as Manuel Azaña put together the "Popular Front," a coalition of left-wing groups and parties, and won a clear majority.

Time, however, was running out for the democracy in Spain. A growing number of forces in

---

[16] Paul Preston, *The Spanish Civil War: Reaction, Revolution & Revenge* (London: Harper Perennial, 2006), p. 79.

[17] Ibid, p. 79.

[18] Ibid, p. 79.

[19] Paul Preston, *The Spanish Civil War: Reaction, Revolution & Revenge* (London: Harper Perennial, 2006), p. 79.

[20] Paul Preston, 'General Franco as a military leader,' *The transactions of the Royal Historical Society*, (4, 1994, pp. 21-41), pp. 25-26.

[21] Francisco J. Romero Salvado, *20th-Century Spain: Politics and Society in Spain, 1898-1998* (Basingstoke: Macmillan, 1999), p. 88.

the country began to move towards the extremes, from the military to fascists, anarchists, and communists. The Republican government, under new Minister of War General Carlos Masquelet, added another affront to Franco's growing list by removing him as Chief of the General Staff and stationing him as commander of the army in the Canary Islands, based in Tenerife.[22] Azaña, Franco's old nemesis, was by now Prime Minister and later President, and it seemed clear the new government leaders wanted Franco as far away as possible from the centers of power.[23] Indalecio Prieto, a leading socialist politician and later Prime Minister, was most acutely aware of Franco's threat. In May 1936, he asserted, "We cannot deny, whatever our political creed, that among the military, in considerable numbers and over wide areas there is subversive ferment, an urge to rise against the Republican regime, not so much surely because of what it now is, but because of what the Popular Front which dominates national policy implies in terms of a near future. General Franco, being young, gifted, having a network of friends in the Army, is the man who at a given moment has it in him to lead such a movement with maximum probable success because of the prestige he enjoys."[24]

The possibilities of a military takeover involving Franco were clearly on the minds of the new leaders in the government, and they had every reason to worry. In fact, a coup was already being planned by the summer of 1936.

The Start of the Civil War

Despite the huge majority of seats won by the Popular Front, key elements in Spain did not support the government. Largo Caballero refused to work with the government, while CEDA and Gil-Robles apparently gave up on democracy and moved closer to military figures, some of which were now plotting a new coup. Therefore, by the summer of 1936, the Republican establishment had been hollowed out, while many politicians, army officers and groups from communists to anarchists to fascists were now looking at non-democratic means of obtaining power.

General Emilio Mola was the focus of the next coup plot.[25] Spain had unquestionably proven difficult, almost impossible, to govern since the Republic was proclaimed in 1931, and numerous risings, strikes, controversial reforms, persecution of the clergy and other political violence such as the Asturias massacre had convulsed the country. Military figures saw a coup as the most effective means of restoring order, and General Mola sought sympathetic army officers to help him launch a national uprising and a swift overthrow of the democracy. The CEDA was supportive, as was the rapidly expanding fascist party, the Falange, led by José Antonio Primo de Rivera. Mola was to direct operations from his base in Pamplona, in the northern province of

[22] Paul Preston, *The Spanish Civil War: Reaction, Revolution & Revenge* (London: Harper Perennial, 2006), p. 94.
[23] Paul Preston, *Franco: A Biography* (London: HarperCollins, 1993), pp. 312–314.
[24] George Hills, *Franco: The Man and His Nation* (London: Robert Hale, 1967), p. 221.
[25] Stanley G. Payne, The Collapse of the Spanish Republic, 1933-1936: Origins of the Civil War, (Yale University Press, 2006), p. 312.

Navarre; the region was a hotbed of Carlism and therefore sympathetic to Mola's objectives. He also liaised with the exiled General Sanjurjo, the head of the 1932 plot, and General Franco, who - clearly distrusted by the Republican government - had been stationed in the Canary Islands.[26]

Mola

The pretext for the uprising came after the assassination of José Calvo Sotelo, the leader of the right-wing opposition in the parliament in Madrid, by police on July 13, 1936. Calvo Sotelo's murder had been retaliation for the killing of José Castillo, a policeman, the previous day by Falangist gunmen.[27] Such was the chaos and violence of Republican Spain. Mola launched his coup on July 17, and with that, the Spanish Civil War had begun.

---

[26] Ibid, p. 312–314.
[27] Tim Reuter, 'Words Can Kill: Class Hatred And The Spanish Civil War', *Forbes*, 8 November 2013, https://www.forbes.com/sites/timreuter/2013/11/08/words-can-kill-class-hatred-and-the-spanish-civil-war/#3698d3312591, [accessed 13 June 2018]

A map showing Nationalist control in pink and Republican control in blue at the start of the war

Franco was inscrutable enough not to have been directly involved in the plot to overthrow the democratically-elected government. His statements before the uprising, however, demonstrated his broad sympathy in favor of its objectives. Franco was also cautious and presumably did not want to commit to enterprises that might fail. In fact, he did not sign on to General Emilio Mola's coup until five days before it started.

Mola shared a number of characteristics with Franco and was five years his senior. He had come from a military background and had been made a Brigadier General one year after Franco, in 1927. Like Franco, he was distrusted by the Popular Front government and was stationed to remote Navarre in Northern Spain near the Pyrenees. Navarre was a conservative stronghold, however, and home of the Carlist movement, which wanted Spain to return to an ultra-conservative monarchy.

Led by General Mola, a significant number of army officers revolted on July 17, and the rebels expected a quick takeover of power. Indeed, many cities across Spain appeared to have fallen within hours. At the same time, however, this was a rebellion against a democratically elected government, which immediately undermined the rebels' case and was one reason for much of the international sympathy for the Republican side. Nevertheless, Mola quickly assumed control in the area around Pamplona where he was based. Navarre was one of Spain's most conservative regions, and in general the greatest support for the uprising occurred in more rural, traditional, and religious areas.[28]

Even after he signed on to join the coup, Franco, still on Tenerife, would need to be transported to Morocco to take charge of his old Legion troops and then travel to mainland Spain. This in fact was arranged through the chartering of a private plane from Britain. It has also been noted that Franco was so cautious - and documents reveal how he had secured a possible exit from the country if things went wrong - about the coup that he landed in mainland Spain only after it was clear that it had, at least partially, succeeded.[29]

Ultimately, rebel sympathizers persuaded the admittedly sympathetic British pilot Cecil Bebb to charter a private plane from Croydon in South London to Tenerife, where he picked up Franco and delivered him to Morocco on July 19. Initially, however, Franco's troops were unable to cross the Strait of Gibraltar to mainland Spain. It was not until almost two weeks later that his troops were transported with the assistance of Nazi Germany, which deployed Junker transport planes.

Franco's Path to Power

At the beginning of the conflict, Franco, who was 43 years old in July 1936, was by no means the leader of the coup. It was Mola who had organized the uprising, and a number of other officers, such as Queipo de Llano, Yagüe, and Sanjurjo, were more senior. Franco's actions during the war would position him as a leader in the eyes of the population sympathetic to the nationalist cause, as well as in the establishment, but fateful events during the war would also bring him to the forefront of the Nationalist cause.

Two of Franco's main rivals, General Mola and General Sanjurjo, died in plane crashes early on in the war. Mola was killed in June 1937, while Sanjurjo died shortly after the rebellion started in 1936. Given how convenient they were for Franco, conspiracy theories cropped up, but there is no concrete evidence Franco played a part in the demise of either.

Moreover, both had lost luster in the eyes of the Nationalists. Mola had displayed the courage to launch the uprising but could not secure a quick victory, and Mola received blame for the early setbacks. Meanwhile, Sanjurjo had been a peripheral figure, attempting a coup in 1932 and being exiled in Portugal after his release from prison. General Queipo de Llano, based in Seville after the initial uprising, was considered by his peers a "lunatic" and was already in his 60s.[30] Other leading military figures such as Generals Goded and Fanjul had been defeated in Madrid and Barcelona, during which they were captured and executed.

---

[28] Michael Seidman, *The Victorious Counterrevolution: The Nationalist Effort in the Spanish Civil War*, (University of Wisconsin Press, 2011), p. 9.

[29] Francisco J. Romero Salvado, *20th-Century Spain: Politics and Society in Spain, 1898-1998* (Basingstoke: Macmillan, 1999), p. 106.

[30] Francisco J. Romero Salvado, *20th-Century Spain: Politics and Society in Spain, 1898-1998* (Basingstoke: Macmillan, 1999), pp. 106-107.

This all left Franco in a strong position within the Nationalist camp, and it was he who improved his personal network by making contact and securing support from Italy and Germany. Although Franco always remained skeptical of the military utility of the Italians, the outside support would be crucial over the course of the war.

Moreover, even as Franco consolidated his position among his supporters, he began to construct a political narrative to match his military supremacy. This involved another slain nationalist, Falangist leader José Antonio Primo de Rivera, the son of the previous dictator. The Falange had, under Primo de Rivera, taken on an increasingly fascist tone before the outbreak of the civil war and had mimicked other European fascist parties. Primo de Rivera thought that his party, and its associated militias, could incite an authoritarian takeover of the country. Nevertheless, the Falange party was still relatively marginal in 1936, even as it had picked up some supporters from the much larger CEDA party of Gil-Robles. Primo de Rivera had actually been arrested in March 1936 for possession of firearms, and at the start of the conflict been moved from Madrid to a prison in Alicante. He was charged with conspiracy against the Republic and executed by firing squad in November 1936. Franco remorselessly used the death of Primo de Rivera for his own propaganda, and over the course of the civil war placed the Falange as the leading political force in the Nationalist zone, with Primo de Rivera as the country's slain martyr. After the civil war, the Falange became the country's sole political party, and when Franco built his infamous monument to the war's soldiers, the Valley of the Fallen, he entombed one figure in its hall: José Antonio Primo de Rivera. It is doubtful, however, that Franco was actually sympathetic to either fascism or Primo de Rivera. In fact, the general had the opportunity to free Primo de Rivera as part of a prisoner exchange in 1936, but he declined, and by all accounts he was never impressed by the Falange leader. Such was the manipulative kind of strategy Franco would use during and after the war.

Of course, for Franco to truly take power, his side still had a war to win, and by the time the Army of Africa arrived, the situation on the ground had changed and battle lines were being drawn. The rebels had managed to take control of a number of cities, mainly in the northwest and southwest of the country. These included the Andalusian cities of Cadiz, Seville, Cordoba, and Granada, as well as towns north of Madrid such as Leon, Valladolid, and Salamanca. Many of these contained populations who were at odds with the aims of the Republican governments and concerned about a socialist revolution. Perhaps most importantly, religious faith was strong in many of these areas. By apparently being in direct confrontation with, or at least turning a blind eye to the persecution of, the clergy, the Republicans had distressed or made enemies of many conservative Spaniards.

On the other hand, the rebels underestimated the levels of resistance to a military takeover. The democratic government came under enormous pressure to start arming the people, and after some procrastination it supplied weapons to ad hoc militia groups. In these early phases of the conflict, this move was highly successful, and volunteer militias beat back the rebels in most of the major population centers, including Barcelona, Madrid and Valencia. In Barcelona, an anarchist unit formed of CNT members proved highly effective. Others, such as the Durruti Column, led by anarchist Buenaventura Durruti, grew to almost 6,000 strong and started to advance towards the city of Zaragoza.[31]

After the initial uprising and counteroffensive by Republican forces, the early battle lines were drawn in the summer of 1936. The Republican government, now led by José Giral following the resignation of Casares Quiroga, had proven surprisingly resilient. In addition to loyalist army officers, it was supported by a variety of left-wing groups, including the anarchists (CNT), the Marxists (POUM, *Partido Obrero de Unificación Marxista*, or Workers' Party of Marxist Unification), the socialists (PSOE), and communists (PCE, *Partido Comunista de Espana*, or Spanish Communist Party). The right-wing forces became known as the Nationalists and included the CEDA, Falangists, Carlists, and Monarchists. One fundamental difference quickly became apparent between the two sides - Mola united his various factions into a cohesive force, while the Republicans remained divided and in many cases antagonistic towards one another.

The years before the Spanish Civil War started were characterized by disorder and political violence. Once the conflict broke out, however, it rapidly turned brutal. Perhaps as a result of the building frustrations and grievances, the civil war almost immediately descended into a cycle of recriminations, massacres and retaliation. This was evident from the earliest weeks of the conflict and was most shocking in terms of civilian executions. The Nationalists committed the so-called "White Terror," while the Republicans indulged in the opposite "Red Terror."[32] For instance, following the Battle of Badajoz, which had been isolated after the Nationalist victory at Merida united the northern and southern zones, upwards of 4,000 civilian and military Republican supporters were executed by firing squads. Federico García Lorca, one of Spain's best-known writers and prominent in the early cultural work of the Republic,[33] was executed in Granada by Nationalist troops and buried in an unmarked grave. His body has never been found.

Inevitably, each side claimed they were avenging atrocities committed by the other, and there were certainly massacres in the Republican zone, often intensifying the previous anti-clerical persecution. It is estimated that over 3,000 priests and nuns were killed in the first two months of the war.

The violence shocked Republican leaders, such as President Azaña, more than the Nationalists. After the early orgy of violence, some semblance of law and order was installed in the Republican zone. In the Nationalist areas, however, retribution was centrally planned and

[31] Alfonso Daniels, 'Meeting Spain's last anarchist', *BBC*, 8 July 2008, http://news.bbc.co.uk/2/hi/americas/7420469.stm, [accessed 1 June 2018]

[32] Stanley G. Payne, *The Spanish Civil War, the Soviet Union, and Communism*, (Yale University Press, 2004), p. 117.

[33] Stanley G. Payne, *The Collapse of the Spanish Republic, 1933-1936: Origins of the Civil War*, (Yale University Press, 2006), p. 139.

actively encouraged by leaders such as Mola and Franco. It is estimated that over the course of the war there were maybe hundreds of thousands murdered in the Nationalist zones, and tens of thousands in the Republican zones. Paul Preston, an eminent historian on the Spanish Civil War, has estimated that 200,000 were executed during the conflict.[34]

Some disaffected leftists saw the outbreak of war as their opportunity to pursue their own revolution. In his novel *Homage to Catalonia*, George Orwell described Barcelona as "startling and overwhelming. It was the first time I had ever been in a town where the working class was in the saddle."[35] Other eastern sections of the country, especially Catalonia, saw anarchist and socialist groups take control of land and towns, thereby imposing their own ideology. Factories, industries, and lands were collectivized and sometimes confiscated. Parts of Spain had effectively become communes by the end of 1936, but the Nationalists also had a number of successes in August and September, including Badajoz, San Sebastian in the Basque Country, and Irun near the French border. The latter allowed Nationalists to monitor the cross-border flow of arms and personnel.

After a meeting between the leading rebel army officers, General Franco was put in ultimate command of the Nationalist troops. His target was the capital city, Madrid. As his troops moved towards the city, however, Franco diverted his forces to Toledo, where Nationalists were under siege. The Republican forces had trapped rebels in the old fortress, known as the Alcázar. In late September, Franco and his Army of Africa "relieved" the Alcázar, beating back the Republicans and forcing them to flee. There was renewed fighting, but the Nationalists held onto the city. There has been some historical debate about the strategic importance of Toledo to either side, of which there was apparently little. Nevertheless, winning and holding Toledo appears to have presented a propaganda triumph for Franco's forces.[36]

Military strategists often target the capital city as key to any victory. Therefore, it was widely assumed a Nationalist victory in Madrid could have ended the war in 1936, and after the relief of the Alcázar, Franco's forces moved on Madrid in October, soon approaching the limits of the city itself. With the Nationalists on the verge of entering the city, the entire resources of the Republic were diverted towards the capital, and in popular memory, the effort to save Madrid was a key moment of solidarity, both within the Republican zones and internationally. Outside Spain, the seemingly imminent capture of Madrid acted as a call to arms to prevent the spread of European fascism and save democracy. Many volunteered from countries all over the world when it appeared Madrid was set to fall to the Nationalists.

The initial movement, however, was within Republican Spain itself. Militias and troops from across the Republic rallied to Madrid's defense, and roads were barricaded by a resolute, but

---

[34] Paul Preston, *The Spanish Holocaust: Inquisition and Extermination in 20th-Century Spain* (W.M. Norton, 2012).

[35] George Orwell, *Homage to Catalonia* (London: Penguin, 1962, originally published 1938), p. 2.

[36] Paul Schue, 'Remember the Alcázar! The creation of Nationalist myths in the Spanish Civil War: The writings of Robert Brasillach', *National Identities*, 10:2, November 2008, pp. 131-147.

fearful, population. Banners appeared across the city defiantly declaring "¡No pasarán!" ("They Shall Not Pass"). Buenaventura Durruti's anarchist column arrived in the city, bringing 4,000 fighters and having already built up a heroic reputation with their exploits in the north of the country. José Miaja, a general loyal to the Republic, took charge of the Madrid Defence Council and prepared for the Nationalist assault. Finally, the first International Brigades arrived in the city, initially consisting of around 2,000 volunteers in support of the Republic.

A banner in Madrid

Victims of an anti-Nationalist purge carried out by Republican loyalists in Madrid

Durruti

The Nationalists attacked the city at the start of November, initially targeting the university area in the west of the city, and the fighting was brutal, often involving hand-to-hand combat. The Republican forces staged a desperate counterattack, and the fighting went on for several weeks. Nationalist forces were supported by Nazi aircraft, the notorious "Condor Legion." The intervention of the "Condor Legion" in this internal conflict enabled thorough testing of the new Third Reich air arm with only slight political repercussions, thereby becoming a trial run without lasting consequences that honed the Luftwaffe into a fast-moving, hard-hitting, advanced instrument of war.

Franco had made the Nationalists' first overtures to Germany on July 22, 1936 as he confronted his Republican opponents for control of Spain. Initial aid consisted of half a dozen Heinkel He 51 biplane fighters, accompanied by 86 Luftwaffe personnel and various items of materiel. 20 Junkers Ju 52 transport aircraft soon joined these, providing Franco's forces with mobility superior to that enjoyed by the Republican armies. The Republicans still possessed numerical superiority, but their chaotic command, general indiscipline, and lack of trained aviators such as those provided to Franco by the "Condor Legion" would soon help tip the balance in Franco's favor.

By December 1936 the Battle for Madrid had ground to a stalemate, with a battle line drawn on the edge of the city that would endure right until the end of the conflict in 1939. The Republican government moved from Madrid to Valencia as a result of the attack, which turned into a siege.[37]

For Republicans, saving Madrid was a huge propaganda victory against the much better equipped and organized Nationalist forces. It helped mobilize international opinion in its favor, and many more volunteers came to Spain as a result of this resistance. The battle was probably the most significant military achievement of the entire war for the Republicans.

The Nationalists, on the other hand, were frustrated by their inability to take Madrid. After the advance had ended, General Franco decided to take another approach to the civil war. Instead of aiming for a quick victory by storming Madrid, the Nationalist forces would slowly grind the Republic down, taking the country city by city, town by town, village by village. In this way Franco was now set on an attritional strategy that would cause far more destruction. After Madrid, Franco also focused more thoroughly on the hearts and minds of the Spanish people. If he could not persuade them of the Nationalist cause, he would force his view of the country on them through the barrel of a gun.

By the end of 1936, Largo Caballero had been installed as Prime Minister and included communists in his cabinet.[38] He managed to bring greater order to the military effort, but the creeping communist influence also alarmed potential allies, such as Britain and France, even as people flooded into Spain from afar to fight. In fact, one of the defining features of the Spanish Civil War was the large numbers (almost 60,000) of international volunteers who joined the fighting, predominantly on the Republican side, shortly after war erupted in summer 1936. The volunteers came mainly, although not exclusively, from other European countries and North America.[39] Many were socialists and communists, but there were also liberals, social democrats, and those who had been persecuted by right-wingers at home, including a German contingent. Many volunteers came to Spain because they were concerned about the spread of fascism and believed they either had to resist fascism then or face it later in a wider conflagration. This latter point was obviously proven right with the outbreak of the Second World War.

The next significant Nationalist gain came in January 1937. As Franco again attempted to take Madrid, which by now had become a siege, Nationalist troops attacked Malaga. The Spanish Nationalist army contingent was backed by almost as many Italian troops. The Republicans, on the other hand, were poorly equipped, with many of its own troops unarmed. The battle was relatively brief, and the Nationalists, led by General Queipo de Llano, declared victory in early February. Mussolini also claimed a propaganda victory due to his troops' involvement (despite being part of the Non-Intervention Committee).

[37] Abel Paz and Paul Sharkey, *Story of the Iron Column: Militant Anarchism in the Spanish Civil War*, (AK Press, 2011), p. 101.

[38] Paul Preston, *Coming of the Spanish Civil War: Reform, Reaction and Revolution in the Second Republic*, (Taylor & Francis Group, 1994), p. 247.

[39] Richard Baxell, *Unlikely Warriors* (London: Aurum Press, 2012), p. 43-76.

By early 1937, Franco's forces had now joined up much of its territory. Spain was almost split in half, with the western section in the hands of the Nationalists and the east governed by the Republic. Across the northern Atlantic coast, however, there was still a significant pocket of territory still under Republican control. This was mostly part of the Basque Country and included the major cities of Bilbao and Santander. The cultural home of the Basques, as well as its administrative capital, was Guernica. After centuries attempting to gain recognition for their language and traditions, the Basques achieved some degree of autonomy under the Second Republic, but it was short-lived.

Ironically, but perhaps fittingly, the most notorious attack of the Spanish Civil War was carried out by the Nazis. Hermann Goering favored greater support to the Spanish Nationalists, so Hitler obliged, reinforcing the Condor Legion under Hugo Sperrle. Due to the He 51's inferiority to the Soviet I-16 fielded by the Republicans, the Nazis quickly phased it out in favor of the Messerschmitt Bf 109, a famous fighter airplane which saw its first combat in 1937. One historian noted the importance of the replacements, writing, "The Bf 109 was introduced into service in 1937 and soon started to equip J./88 in Spain. Powered by a Junkers Jumo 210 engine, the Bf 109B represented the cutting edge of aircraft technology. Armed with two MG 17 7.9 mm machine guns its introduction proved to be an immediate success and the Bf 109B quickly proved to be a better fighter than the I-16. [...] the 109 pilots chose to base their tactics on a two-aircraft formation, called a Rotte, to give more flexibility." (Jacobs, 2014, 17-18).

Messerschmitt Bf 109

Capable of flying at 250 miles per hour and with a service ceiling of 30,000 feet, the Messerschmitt Bf 109 would sweep the Spanish skies of opposition and gave the Condor Legion air superiority. At the same time, the Germans honed their tactics for future conflicts. Werner Molders, the Third Reich's first air ace with 14 victories, introduced the four-aircraft "Schwarm" as the basic Luftwaffe tactical unit. By this time, 20,000 Germans fought on Franco's side, including 200 fighter pilots known as "Jagdflieger" ("hunting-fliers"). They formed the hard core of the Luftwaffe during its later Polish adventure.

Molders

The conflict also revealed the potential of the Junkers Ju 87 Stuka dive-bomber. Unfortunately, but predictably, the Germans did not limit themselves to pummeling their communist-backed military adversaries into submission. On April 26, 1937, a German bombing raid targeted Guernica in an attempt to break the will of the population and allow the Nationalists to capture the remaining Republican areas in the region. The order was given by the Nationalist high command but was carried out by the "Condor Legion." Starting in the late afternoon, the German planes destroyed the Basque's ancient city, solely by targeting civilians since the town had no specific military importance. Hundreds were killed and many more fled. As one writer aptly put it, the Germans "introduced another innovation: the Fascist terror raid. On April 26 [they] attacked the Basque town of Guernica with He-111 and Ju-52 bombers, which dropped incendiary and high-explosive bombs, while He-51 fighters strafed the fleeing and unarmed civilian inhabitants, clearly in violation of international law. Some 1,654 civilians were killed and 889 were wounded. 'Guernica,' Fletcher wrote later, '...has since become a synonym for Fascist brutality in Spain.'" (Mitcham, 2007, 48). Thanks to attacks like Guernica, Luftwaffe personnel honed the Stuka's dive-bombing methods and provided useful feedback on necessary technical improvements for later marks of the aircraft, while simultaneously having a bit of fun with their unusual unit insignia. One historian explained that "the activity of a few Ju 87s in Spain permitted the fine tuning of 'pinpoint' bombing techniques in an environment less dangerous than would have been found in a conflict such as the Polish campaign, and thereby steal a bit of a march on history. […] the squadron mascot was a charming little piglet who waltzed about with a model of a bomb around its neck." (Laureau, 2000, 195).

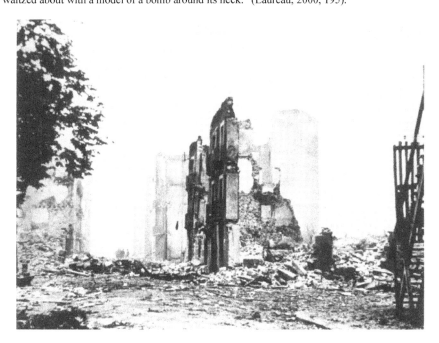

A picture of the ruins of Guernica

General Mola's troops took Guernica three days after the raid and soon after commenced the final offensive to take the rest of the Basque Country.[40] The Nationalists may have been hoping to keep news of the civilian bombing at Guernica quiet, but thanks to the reports of journalist George Steer, events were quickly conveyed around the world.[41] Most were appalled by the Guernica massacre and concluded that the Nationalists were more egregious in their methods than the Republicans.

1937 witnessed many of the key battles of the civil war, and the pattern established during this year governed the final outcome of the conflict. By this point, the Republican army was more centrally organized and decided to launch a number of offensives. The balance of power was still relatively finely balanced. Franco's forces controlled approximately half of the country, but even though the Nationalists occupied a number of cities such as Seville, Malaga, Cadiz, and Cordoba, they had failed to take the major population centers of Barcelona, Valencia, Bilbao, and Madrid. If the Republicans could successfully advance in the coming series of campaigns, the war very well could have been won.

When several Republican offensives were comprehensively halted over the final months of 1937, the Nationalists moved to complete their takeover of the North Atlantic coast. The pocket of Republican resistance in the northeast of the country had looked vulnerable ever since early Nationalist gains at the start of the war, and during 1937 it looked ever more isolated, particularly after the terror bombing of Guernica and the takeover of Bilbao. The Republican forces, made up predominantly of Basque soldiers, were now hopelessly outnumbered. The offensives at Segovia, Huesca, Brunete, Zaragoza and Belchite had stalled the final victory on the Atlantic coast, but only marginally. Santander fell on September 26, and the last desperate refugees attempted to leave the country by sea. In October, Asturias, where the miners had stood up to the right-wing government and had been massacred by Franco three years earlier, was finally overrun by Nationalist forces. The consequences were severe for those who had held out in Asturias - around 1,000 Republicans were believed to have been executed in the aftermath.

With that, Franco had consolidated control of Spain's northwest and the Atlantic coast. He could now turn his attention to the eastern portion of the country. There were fears that the Nationalists would soon move on Valencia, and although this didn't happen for another year, the Republican government abandoned the city at the end of October and moved to Barcelona.

---

[40] *The Spanish Civil War: A Modern Tragedy*, edited by George R. Esenwein, (Routledge, 2005), p. 209.
[41] David Boyd Haycock, *I Am Spain: The Spanish Civil War and the Men and Women who went to Fight Fascism*, (Brecon: Old Street Publishing, 2012), p. 223.

A map of the lines in 1938, with the Republican forces split in two

The Republican government had options available to it in the summer of 1938 as it sought to stave off complete defeat. Its leaders still held out hope that the democratic forces, Britain and France, would intervene on its behalf; Nazi Germany was posing a growing threat to European security, and many politicians in Britain and France were coming around to the reality that they would have to confront Hitler. In this respect, Spain may have been saved if Britain and France had taken a stand against the fascist powers in 1938. The second option was a negotiated settlement, and the Republican government did start to pursue this option in 1938. Franco, however, was steadfast in his refusal to negotiate. He was determined to eradicate left-wing influence in Spain.

In the absence of those alternatives, the Republicans could only continue to fight, and in mid-1938 the Republicans launched one final offensive that led to the last major battle of the Spanish Civil War. The River Ebro runs from the Pyrenees in the north of Spain past Zaragoza in Aragon and all the way into the Mediterranean Sea, south of Barcelona. If the Republicans could cross the River Ebro, they could potentially cut through the Nationalist lines that currently divided Barcelona with Valencia, but it was certainly an ambitious plan. Meanwhile, Franco was planning an assault on Valencia, instead of the apparently more straightforward attack on Barcelona.

The move towards Valencia was the last great Republican effort of the war across the River Ebro. General Vicente Rojo, one of the most respected Republican military figures of the war, led this attack, which consisted of around 80,000 men and virtually all the remaining planes and heavy armaments the Republicans had.[42] It was a desperate final throw of the dice.

Republican anti-aircraft artillery positioned during the battle

The Battle of the Ebro was the longest and largest engagement of the Spanish Civil War, lasting from July-November. Under the cover of darkness during the evening of July 24, Republican commandos crossed the Ebro and cut some of the Nationalist communication lines. The initial units of the Republican army then progressed some 25 kilometers towards Ganesa. The morale of the Republicans was suddenly lifted, while the Nationalist troops grew anxious, having previously thought the end of the conflict was close at hand.[43]

As with so many of the key battles of the civil war, however, early Republican gains were halted by the Nationalists, who then ground their opponents down, and finally retook the lost

---

[42] *The Spanish Civil War: A Modern Tragedy*, edited by George R. Esenwein, (Routledge, 2005), p. 232.
[43] Ibid.

land. Between August and October, the area around the Ebro River was the site of desperate and bloody clashes.[44] The Republicans were aware that the very existence of their state hung on the outcome of the battle. Ultimately, however, the Republicans were slowly weakened by the heavy bombardment of the Nationalists, including their overwhelming superiority in the skies. By November 16, the Nationalists had pushed back the Republicans past their initial positions and the Battle of the Ebro was over. Both sides, in particular the Republicans, had suffered huge losses, estimated between 50,000 and 110,000 casualties.

It was now clear that the Republicans had no chance of military victory in the war, and many leaders began looking for a way out, or at least an end to the fighting. Making matters worse, most of the Republican leadership was now in Barcelona, in the pocket of Catalonia that looked ever more isolated. The Republic still had a large swath of territory between Madrid and Valencia in the center and southeast of the country, but it was now a matter of when, not if, Franco achieved his final victory.

While the Battle of the Ebro was still raging, at the end of September 1938, the European powers met at the Munich Conference, which turned out to be one of the most infamous moments of the 20th century. In addition to paving the way for World War II by abandoning Czechoslovakia to the Nazis and solidifying the concept of "appeasement" as geopolitical folly for decades to come, Munich also had implications for the Spanish Civil War. Most importantly, it showed Franco that Britain and France had no stomach for military confrontation and therefore seemed highly unlikely to intervene in Spain at all. In the same vein, Munich also affected the Republican strategy, because without the possibility of French or British assistance, the Republic was effectively at the mercy of Franco and the fascist powers. Munich also demonstrated that the democracies had been ill-advised in their neglect of the Spanish rebellion. By refusing to intervene, and by turning a blind eye to Italy and Germany's interference, Britain and France had perpetuated the appeasement strategy in Spain. This had emboldened Hitler and Mussolini, and now events were much more serious. Despite the "peace in our time" rhetoric of Chamberlain, it was becoming alarmingly clear to many Europeans that a major confrontation was looming in Europe in the late 1930s, one that would dwarf the Spanish Civil War.

Just before Christmas 1938, Franco finally launched his offensive in Catalonia. Barcelona had been a key city throughout the years of the Republic and the civil war.[45] Having reveled in a degree of autonomy in 1931, Barcelona was the site of the Catalan provincial government. It was here that Lluís Companys had declared independence – albeit within Spain – in 1934, and it had been one of the focal points of resistance against the rebellion in 1936. Barcelona had been an anarchist stronghold from the beginning of the war, and it had been the scene of inter-Republican

[44] Michael Kerr, 'Homage to the fallen of Catalonia, 80 years on', *The Telegraph*, 17 July 2016, https://www.telegraph.co.uk/travel/destinations/europe/spain/catalonia/articles/spanish-civil-war-homage-to-the-fallen-of-catalonia/, [accessed 29 May 2018]

[45] Stephen Burgen, 'Barcelona and the Spanish civil war', *The Guardian*, 22 July 2012, https://www.theguardian.com/travel/2012/jul/22/barcelona-spanish-civil-war-travel, [accessed 13 June 2018]

fighting as the socialists attempted to bring all the factions under its control. Since the end of 1937, Barcelona had been the seat of the Republican government itself. Now it faced almost certain defeat at the hands of Franco's Nationalists, many of whom held a special contempt for Catalonia.[46] For Francoists, the region embodied everything that they despised about the Republican era, namely separatism, anarchism, and social revolution. The reckoning was sure to be harsh when the dust settled in Catalonia.

As it turned out, Franco's Catalonia Offensive was quicker and less bloody than many others in the Spanish Civil War. The Republicans were already a spent force, and the Nationalists had over 300,000 men to confront an enemy that, despite having a sizeable number of troops, lacked weapons and hardware.

The Nationalists moved quickly through Catalonia and had taken Barcelona by January 26, 1939. Many in the city, including the military and political leadership, fled the city and headed towards the border with France. The roads were packed with about half a million refugees as the Nationalists moved ever closer to the border, and many of the key political figures - Manuel Azaña, Juan Negrín, Lluís Companys, and head of the military, Vicente Rojo - crossed over into France at the start of February. Franco's forces reached the border on February 9, 1939. Three weeks later, in a bitter pill for the Republicans, Britain and France recognized the Nationalists as the legitimate government of Spain despite almost a third of its territory still being out of its control. Not surprisingly, Franco rebuffed Negrín's desperate attempts to broker an armistice or negotiated end to the conflict and instead sought an unconditional surrender.

Things went from bad to worse for the remaining Republican resistance at the start of March. In Madrid, Republican Colonel Segismundo Casado launched a coup against the civilian government, ousting Negrín and immediately attempting to forge an agreement with Franco. The Nationalist leader again refused. Three weeks later, the Nationalists launched their final offensive. By this time the Spanish people were exhausted, tired of war, and longed for peace. The final battles lasted just five days as the Nationalists cut through Republican territory with ease. Refugees attempted to flee from the eastern ports of Valencia, Alicante, and Cartagena. Many had not escaped by the time the whole of Spain had been taken by the Nationalists on March 31. The following day, on April 1, Franco claimed victory. The Spanish Civil War was over.

---

[46] Paul Preston, *The Spanish Civil War: Reaction, Revolution & Revenge* (London: Harper Perennial, 2006), pp. 294-295.

Franco and other Nationalist leaders during the civil war

World War II

Even after the civil war was over, there was still plenty of violence taking place across Spain. As World War II entered its early stages, Franco wreaked a terrible vengeance on those who had fought for, assisted, served, or collaborated with the Republic. An estimated half a million Republicans were imprisoned after the war, and it is believed that perhaps 50,000 were executed. Concentration camps were established throughout Spain and were packed full of Republican prisoners. Franco wanted to stamp out any possibility of resistance to his rule, but even still, there were armed groups that waged a low-level conflict against the Nationalist government well into the 1940s.

As the civil war drew to a close, most of the Republican leadership went into exile in France, and then Mexico. Manuel Azaña died only months after the end of the civil war in France. Juan Negrín technically remained Republican leader until 1945, as head of the "Spanish Republican government in exile," based in Paris and then Mexico City. Lluís Companys, President of the Catalan Parliament, also went into exile, but he was still in France in 1940 when the Nazis occupied that country. The Nazis captured Companys and extradited him back to Spain, where Franco's retribution was predictably severe.[47] Companys was kept in solitary confinement for

---

[47] Charles Bremner, 'Political extraditions are far from straightforward', *The Times*, 27 March 2018, https://www.thetimes.co.uk/article/political-extraditions-are-far-from-straightforward-hbfckxg60, [accessed 13 June 2018]

five weeks, tortured, and subsequently put on trial for just one hour before being given a death sentence. Ironically, Companys death sentence was for the crime of military rebellion, which he apparently committed by opposing the Nationalists' military coup. He was executed by firing squad on October 15, 1940. Shouting "For Catalonia!" before his death, Lluís Companys is still revered as a hero by Catalan nationalists to this day.

Despite the fact his rule was the byproduct of a coup, Franco and his regime, while not securing full international acceptance for another 20 years, quickly gained some degree of legitimacy. Britain and France recognized Franco's government in short order, another insult to the Republican regime that had requested support from other democracies during the civil war, and the Axis powers were only too happy to welcome Spain into their burgeoning fascist club. Franco's win had been a major propaganda victory for Hitler and Mussolini, and it certainly filled them with confidence - in terms of military tactics and hardware - should another European war break out. The nationalist triumph also demonstrated to the Axis powers that they could expect little resistance from the democracies that were hamstrung by public opinion, which wanted to avoid war. Dictatorships had no such restraints.

Franco had made much of his religious credentials, and he had repeatedly asserted that the civil war was a battle between Christian civilization and the barbarous, godless communist invaders. He was therefore delighted to receive a message from Pope Pius XII on March 19, 1936 sending Franco his blessing.[48]

On August 8, 1939, Franco was granted essentially unrestrained power by the new and largely ceremonial legislative body. In a few short years Franco had gone from establishment army officer to the ultimate ruler of Spain. Indeed, the seemingly restrained and cautious figure had proven to be a consummate strategist and highly political.

Given how devastated Spain was by the war, it made perfect sense that at the outset of World War II, Franco played a cautious role by aligning himself with the Axis, but without committing troops to the fighting. This brought costs and benefits. Nazi Germany, in particular, was frustrated by Franco's lack of full cooperation, but it nevertheless provided breathing space for Spain, which was exhausted after its civil war. It also helped that Germany made critical gains at the start of 1940, capturing Norway, Belgium, and then France. Britain seemed cornered by June 1940 and on the brink of capitulation.

Spain remained officially neutral throughout World War II, but as part of the quid pro quo for German assistance during the civil war, Franco provided the Nazis with raw materials, most notably iron and copper. Hitler met with Franco in October 1940, while the Nazis were at the peak of their power, at the French town of Hendaye. Hitler attempted to persuade Franco to join the fighting, but the Spanish dictator stubbornly resisted. Instead, Franco cooperated with the

---

[48] Paul Preston, *Franco: A Biography* (London: HarperCollins, 1993), p. 322.

Nazis diplomatically and logistically, without engaging more deeply in the war. It is believed that the two strongmen intensely disliked each other.[49] Hitler later told Mussolini that "rather than go through that again, I would prefer to have three or four teeth taken out."[50] Franco, for his part, came to realize that Hitler had little respect for Spain or its leader, and as a result the relationship began to cool.

Franco with SS officials Karl Wolff and Heinrich Himmler

That aside, Franco sought to capitalize on the opportunities the shifting European balance of power presented, in particular at Gibraltar.[51] Franco - under pressure from the nationalists in the Falange - sought to capture Gibraltar, which had been under British control since the early 18th century and represented an affront to Spanish nationalists. Thus, he made plans to invade, but he was frustrated by the stubborn reluctance of the British, who refused to make peace with the Axis powers.[52] As a result, the plan was permanently postponed, but the Gibraltar issue became a long-running sore under his regime. He closed the border between Gibraltar and the mainland in

---

[49] Fiona Govan, 'Franco 'feared Hitler would kidnap him', *The Telegraph*, 28 November 2008, https://www.telegraph.co.uk/news/worldnews/europe/spain/3533400/Franco-feared-Hitler-would-kidnap-him.html, [accessed 10 June 2018]

[50] Paul Preston, *Franco: A Biography* (London: HarperCollins, 1993), p. 399.

[51] Ibid, p. 358.

[52] Francisco J. Romero Salvado, *20th-Century Spain: Politics and Society in Spain, 1898-1998* (Basingstoke: Macmillan, 1999), p. 133.

1969, and it was not reopened until after Franco's death.

The real focus of Franco's early years in power was on concentrating power and eliminating all traces of opposition to his regime. He allowed the Falange party to gain prominence,[53] either merging with other right-wing elements or banning hostile ones.[54] Any semblance of separatism, independence and uniqueness in the regions (most notably in Catalonia and the Basque Country), was stamped out. Franco's regime sought to extinguish the remnants of the Republican Army, parts of which mounted a low-level resistance for years after the civil war had ended, and naturally Franco remained wary of the exiled Republican leadership.

The Cold War Years

If the loose alliance with the fascist powers at the start of the Second World War had provided some benefits for Franco, the defeat of Germany and Italy left Spain in an isolated position. Indeed, as the Allies moved towards their final victory, some considered overthrowing Franco as part of the fascist coalition in Europe. After all, Franco had initiated one of the first moves that led to the European conflict and was clearly closely aligned with Hitler and Mussolini. Ultimately, however, the exhausted Allies opted not to deal with Franco, if only because they were warily drawing ideological lines between Western Europe and Eastern Europe.

Franco was nonetheless left with few friends during the 1940s, unable to join the newly founded international organizations and rebuild the Spanish economy. The Soviet Union, in particular, applied diplomatic pressure to Spain in international forums, and it was the last major power to recognize Franco's Spain

Franco's Spain was conservative and reactionary. It was also supposedly monarchist, and indeed the *Caudillo* reinstated the monarchy in 1947, 16 years after its abolition at the start of the Second Republic. Despite this move, however, Franco did not place a monarch on the throne, instead making himself effectively regent for life.[55] It was a typical Franco move, confirmed through a "referendum," and he managed to pacify the strong monarchist sentiments amongst his supporters while simultaneously reinforcing and extending his own personal power.

The early years of Franco's rule did have a fascist veneer, at least superficially (for instance around Franco's cult of personality),[56] but this changed over time to become a more orthodox autocratic mode of governance. The 1942 "Organic Law" consolidated the early changes in Franco's Spain, confirming the *Caudillo* as head of every meaningful institution and locating the head of the pliant *Cortes* (parliament) in Madrid. The Falange was now the country's only legal

---

[53] Paul Preston, *The Spanish Civil War: Reaction, Revolution & Revenge* (London: Harper Perennial, 2006), p. 322.
[54] Paul Preston, *Franco: A Biography* (London: HarperCollins, 1993), p. 337.
[55] Tobias Buck, 'Facing up to Franco: Spain 40 years on', *Financial Times*, 8 May 2015, https://www.ft.com/content/5e4e6aac-f42f-11e4-99de-00144feab7de, [accessed 22 June 2018]
[56] Nigel Townson, *Is Spain Different? A Comparative Look at the 19th and 20th Centuries* (Sussex Academic Press, 2015), p. 137.

political party, and any remnants of regional autonomy were suffocated. When Serrano Súñer attempted to move the Falange closer to the Nazi model, however, Franco sidelined his brother-in-law.[57] Spanish was declared the country's official and only language, while regional customs, languages, and legislative offices were proscribed in Francoist Spain.

During the 1940s, Franco attempted to make Spain economically self-sufficient, or autarchic. An economic model of autarchy was a common fascist aspiration and maybe logical for extreme nationalists.[58] It nevertheless proved disastrous for the country, which remained unreconstructed after the civil war and left many of its inhabitants poor.[59] As a result, Spain started to see waves of its people migrate in search of better economic opportunities and relief from the stifling political environment in the country.

Franco's tight grip on power went through several stages, becoming less violent during the 1950s and changing again in the late 1960s as his health went into decline. That allowed others to put in place the foundations that would eventually see a peaceful transition to democracy.

The end of Spain's complete isolation, however, was the result of the hardening of attitudes between the post-war superpowers and the rapid development of the Cold War. Suddenly, Franco's strictly anti-communist regime appeared to offer benefits to the Western democracies.[60] It was a similar story for a number of other European dictatorships, such as Portugal, Greece, and Turkey, and over the course of the 1950s and 1960s, Spain built a relationship with the United States and the European democracies. This led to security cooperation, then limited diplomatic and economic collaboration, but it also meant that liberal democratic states would have to turn a blind eye to Franco's excesses.

Monuments were built across the country to memorialize the Nationalist troops, while the Republican soldiers and civilians who died were forgotten. Soon after the civil war had ended, in 1940, work began on a huge shrine in honor of the Nationalist dead. Near Madrid, the *Valle de los Caídos*, or the Valley of the Fallen, was not completed until 1959. A giant monument and crypt that housed Franco's remains after his death, the *Valle* is the site of 40,000 Nationalist fighters' remains. It is believed that the monument was built using the slave labor of thousands of Republican prisoners.

---

[57] Tatjana Pavlovic, *Despotic Bodies and Transgressive Bodies: Spanish Culture from Francisco Franco to Jesus Franco* (State University of New York Press, 2002), p. 14.

[58] Adrian Shubert, *A Social History of Modern Spain* (Taylor & Francis Group, 1990), p. 206.

[59] Tatjana Pavlovic, *Despotic Bodies and Transgressive Bodies: Spanish Culture from Francisco Franco to Jesus Franco* (State University of New York Press, 2002), p. 11.

[60] Nigel Townson, *Is Spain Different? A Comparative Look at the 19th and 20th Centuries* (Sussex Academic Press, 2015), p. 140.

The *Valle de los Caídos*

The economy, however, continued to be a problem for Franco. The country was excluded from much international trade and was only partially industrialized. Wages in 1951 were still only 60% of what they had been in real terms in 1936, and Spain's GDP per capita lagged far behind other European countries.[61] Franco's economic policies had been woefully inadequate, and due to a balance of payments crisis, inflation increased in the 1950s.

It was at this point that Western countries could have forced political reform, in exchange for foreign exchange or diplomatic acceptance, on Spain. By the end of the 1950s, the country was running out of foreign currency reserves and had serious economic problems. Spain was in fact perilously close to bankruptcy.[62] Cold War priorities, however, took precedence for the United States, and the American obsession with curbing communism probably saved Franco. After his election in November 1952, President Dwight Eisenhower sought to improve relations with Spain as part of his Cold War strategy, and the two countries soon signed the 1953 Pact of Madrid, which improved military and trade ties. The United States constructed four military

---

[61] Paul Preston, *The Spanish Civil War: Reaction, Revolution & Revenge* (London: Harper Perennial, 2006), p. 322.
[62] Adrian Shubert, *A Social History of Modern Spain* (Taylor & Francis Group, 1990), p. 207.

bases in Spain, as part of its attempt to contain the Soviet Union and its allies, and provided Franco's regime with huge amounts of aid, possibly up to $500 million per year, starting the following year.[63]

The rapprochement with the United States led to a cascade of acceptance and benefits for Franco's regime. Spain was admitted to the United Nations in 1955, then the OECD (Organisation for Economic Co-operation and Development) and a host of international economic organisations. President Eisenhower visited Franco in Madrid in 1959, further consolidating the new relationship.[64]

Franco himself took a step during this period that did benefit the country's economy by shifting power to a group of unlikely reformers. A reshuffle in 1957 allowed a group of ministers to gain influence, particularly in economic policy, with links to the Opus Dei, an ultra-conservative sect of the Roman Catholic Church.[65] The Opus group, led by Laureano López Rodó, attempted to modernize the Spanish economy and open it to trade while retaining authoritarian sentiments on politics and social policy.

Having joined the IMF in 1958, Spain put in place policies that liberalized trade and controlled inflation, thereby stabilizing the financial environment and encouraging foreign investment.[66] Spain could now become a thriving tourist destination, particularly for other Europeans who flocked to the coastal resorts that soon appeared, such as the Costa del Sol, Costa Brava, and Costa Blanca. The results were spectacular, and Spain's economy grew an average of 7.5% a year between 1961 and 1973. Naturally, Franco was quick to claim credit for the economic boom.[67]

As Spain rebounded, Franco delegated some responsibilities to others during this period, many of whom pressed to make other liberalizing reforms, but he rejected most of them (albeit with less force). Reformist ministers, for instance, wanted changes to the so-called "Organic Law." A new document was presented to the Spanish parliament in November 1966 that slightly constrained the power of the *Caudillo*, which would have been unthinkable 20 years earlier, but Franco by then was spending more time pursuing favorite pastimes like hunting.[68] He also began to show symptoms of Parkinson's disease.[69]

One curious policy of the Franco regime was its approach to its colonies. Franco had made his

[63] Nigel Townson, *Is Spain Different? A Comparative Look at the 19th and 20th Centuries* (Sussex Academic Press, 2015), p. 141.
[64] Francisco J. Romero Salvado, *20th-Century Spain: Politics and Society in Spain, 1898-1998* (Basingstoke: Macmillan, 1999), p. 146.
[65] Ibid, p. 147.
[66] Ibid, p. 148.
[67] Ibid, p. 149.
[68] Paul Preston, *Franco: A Biography* (London: HarperCollins, 1993), pp. 724-725.
[69] Paul Preston, *Franco: A Biography* (London: HarperCollins, 1993), p. 729.

name fighting in the Rif War in Spanish Morocco and utilized the Army of Africa during the civil war. As a Spanish nationalist, it would have seemingly made sense for Franco to try to consolidate or increase control over Spain's colonial possessions, and he had wanted to take back sovereignty of Gibraltar during the Second World War. However, the difficult international environment in which Spain found itself during the 1950s, as well as the country's relative economic weakness, compelled Franco to dispense with the African territories.[70] Decolonization was another step that gradually led to more acceptance of Franco's regime in the eyes of Western countries.[71] After French-controlled Morocco gained independence in 1956, Franco handed over the Spanish section to King Mohammed V. The remaining enclaves in North Africa were gradually decolonized, and in 1968, Franco also surrendered control of Equatorial Guinea.[72]

Life in Franco's Spain

After the civil war, Franco maintained his divisive tactics and never seriously attempted to reconcile the people of Spain. He felt obliged to satisfy the various groups that had supported him during the conflict, namely the church, the military, the aristocratic landowners, and the Falange.[73]

Franco and the system he put in place maintained a deeply conservative outlook. Women were given few rights and were expected to stay at home and bring up children. Birth control and divorce would be illegal in Spain until 1978, but even as Franco's administration offered perks and incentives to have large families, the birthrate actually went into decline in the 25 years after the end of the civil war.[74] Women lost political rights and the suffrage that they had achieved during the Republic, and the role of the Catholic Church was reinforced. The Franco regime reinstalled the civic code of 1889, which made married women essentially subordinate to their husbands.[75] The number of women who married increased dramatically, from 47% in 1940 to 59% in 1965, demonstrating that Franco's social environment had some impact on behavior.[76]

The Catholic Church took on a central position in Franco's Spain, and the dictator used the institution for ideological validity.[77] Franco had a particular view of conservative traditions

[70] Nigel Townson, *Is Spain Different? A Comparative Look at the 19th and 20th Centuries* (Sussex Academic Press, 2015), p. 151.

[71] René Pélissier, 'Spain's Discreet Decolonization', *Foreign Affairs*, April 1965, https://www.foreignaffairs.com/articles/equatorial-guinea/1965-04-01/spains-discreet-decolonization, [accessed 22 June 2018]

[72] Spain still has colonial possessions, for instance Ceuta, Melilla and Spanish Sahara in North West Africa. One could also consider the Canary Islands as remnants of the Spanish Empire.

[73] Victor Alba, *Transition in Spain: From Franco to Democracy* (New Brunswick: Transaction Books, translated by Barbara Lotito, 1978), p. 171.

[74] Adrian Shubert, *A Social History of Modern Spain* (Taylor & Francis Group, 1990), p. 212.

[75] Adrian Shubert, *A Social History of Modern Spain* (Taylor & Francis Group, 1990), p. 214.

[76] Ibid, p. 212.

[77] Chris Grocott, Review of 'Fear and Progress: Ordinary Lives in Franco's Spain, 1939-1975' by Antonio Cazorla Sánchez, *Reviews in History*, July 2010, http://www.history.ac.uk/reviews/review/936, [accessed 25 June 2018]

within Spain. For instance, customs such as bullfighting and flamenco were promoted, although the latter was essentially rooted in the region of Andalusia, while other regional traditions were vigorously suppressed. Censorship was widespread in Franco's Spain although this diminished partly towards the end of the general's life.

In some respects, the changes in the second half of Franco's rule can be seen as a triumph of liberalism and the results of increasingly close ties to the West. Liberal economic reforms implemented in the 1950s forced profound changes on what was a backward country. In 1960, around 40% of the workforce still toiled on the land in the agricultural sector, but by 1970 this had fallen to 15%.[78] Spain started to actively participate and benefit from the global economy, for instance in automobile manufacturing. The car company SEAT was set up in 1950, producing approximately 36,000 vehicles a year in 1960. By 1973, car factories in Spain produced 700,000 vehicles a year, a phenomenal increase.[79] Many workers moved from rural areas to larger cities in search of new, better paying jobs. This also stimulated a rising middle class, which sought more representation and stronger employment rights. Trade unions, which were crushed in the 1940s, were given more freedom from the late 1950s, and by the time Franco died, strikes were common in Spain.[80] As Nigel Townson noted, "The sweeping economic, social and cultural transformation of Spain during the 1960s and early 1970s created both a society and a State that were very different from those of the 1940s and 1950s."[81]

Economic growth and political oppression had managed to pacify much of Spain in the decades after the civil war, and to the outside observer Franco's regime was stable. The brutal policies of Franco's regime, however, inevitably brought about fierce opposition among certain constituents. This became most acute in the Basque Country. The Second Spanish Republic had granted a degree of autonomy to the regions, several of which had agitated for greater self-rule for centuries. Although these regions were often very different politically - the Galicians and Basques, for instance, were conservative and traditional societies, whereas Catalonia was more industrialized and was home to Europe's largest anarchist movement - the areas had some elements in common, especially when it came to fighting the Nationalists during the civil war.

Franco's retribution had been particularly vicious in the independently-minded regions, crushing any political, legal, linguistic, and cultural signs of separatism. Executions and imprisonment in the regions were also particularly numerous. It is perhaps unsurprising, therefore, that armed groups formed to resist Franco's rule. The most infamous, formed in 1959, was *Euskadi Ta Askatasuna* ("Basque Country and Freedom"), which went on to become one of Europe's most notorious terrorist groups.[82] It was not until a decade later, however, in 1968, that

---

[78] Adrian Shubert, *A Social History of Modern Spain* (Taylor & Francis Group, 1990), p. 208.
[79] Ibid, p. 208.
[80] Nigel Townson, *Is Spain Different? A Comparative Look at the 19th and 20th Centuries* (Sussex Academic Press, 2015), p. 151.
[81] Nigel Townson, *Is Spain Different? A Comparative Look at the 19th and 20th Centuries* (Sussex Academic Press, 2015), p. 151.

ETA committed its first attack against the regime when its members shot dead an officer of the *Guardia Civil* (the elite Spanish police). They also assassinated the head of San Sebastian's secret police, Melitón Manzanas, who was a well-known practitioner of torture in the Basque region.

After that, both sides escalated their tactics. The Franco regime attempted to snuff out the armed organization, while ETA committed ever more serious attacks. As it turned out, the armed Basque separatist movement would outlasted Franco.

Franco's Final Years

Franco's health deteriorated during the late 1960s, but he had effectively handed over control of the country's economy to reformers during the previous decade, yielding spectacular results that were dubbed the "Spanish Miracle."[83] The country had started to become more open, spurred in part by its embrace of foreign tourism,[84] even as Franco himself attempted to maintain a tight grip on political events and continued taking an ultra-conservative approach to social affairs. He only partially succeeded. Spain was drifting towards greater liberalism and progressive values despite Franco's best efforts to consolidate his clearly arcane vision of Spanish society.

Franco finally nominated a successor in 1969. His choice was Prince Juan Carlos, who Franco believed would maintain Franco's policies after the *Caudillo* was gone. Ironically, Franco could have named Juan Carlos's father, Infante Juan, as his successor, but he feared Infante Juan was too liberal.

---

[82] Claude Canellas, Sonya Dowsett, Isla Binnie, 'Basque militants ETA surrender arms in end to decades of conflict', *Reuters*, 7 April 2017, https://www.reuters.com/article/us-spain-eta-idUSKBN1790YK, [accessed 25 June 2018]

[83] Paul Preston, *The Spanish Civil War: Reaction, Revolution & Revenge* (London: Harper Perennial, 2006), p. 323.

[84] Stanley G. Payne, *The Franco Regime, 1936–1975* (University of Wisconsin Press, 2011), p. 458.

Juan Carlos

Infante Juan

As part of the succession plans, the prince had to spend time in all three armed forces, and Franco made it clear that he anticipated Juan Carlos would continue his project. The *Caudillo* was a secretive and cunning man who had reached the zenith of power in Spain through carefully planned, strategic moves, and it is safe to assume that Franco would not have bequeathed the succession to Juan Carlos if he had suspected a rapid transition to liberal democracy. However, historians have speculated that the prince planned to liberalize Spain all along. Paul Preston noted that "it is difficult to avoid the conclusion that the Prince, having learned from his mentor how to keep his cards close to his chest, planned all along to deceive him by working for the transition to democracy after his death."[85]

Indeed, external events would also lead to liberalism. The momentum of the economic boom was lost somewhat after the oil price hike of 1973 and its related inflation. This was an issue which afflicted many advanced economies, and Spain was no different. A sense of economic crisis coincided with the end of Franco's rule, and a global recession following the oil shock

---

[85] Ibid, p. 743.

caused the Spanish economy to stagnate. Inflation rose markedly, approaching 30% in the middle of the decade.

For Spain, however, both the economic and political developments progressed in similar directions. The economy picked up again later in the 1970s, inflation came down, and GDP growth boomed after the country joined the European Community in 1986.

In 1973, at the age of 80, Franco had given up the role of Prime Minister in favor of Admiral Luis Carrero Blanco. A long-time confidant and ally of Franco, Carrero appeared to be a safe choice for the *Caudillo*, but with Franco now in poor health, a battle for influence began behind the scenes, portrayed by historians as one between hard-line Francoists and more liberal reformers.

Carrero

Carrero, closer to Francoism, appeared to be in position to succeed the general until he was assassinated by an ETA bomb in December 1973, a little after six months in office. The apparently more liberal Carlos Arias Navarro, who had in fact been involved in the White Terror, took over as Prime Minister, shifting the balance of power away from the conservatives mainly because his advisors favored a break from Francoism.[86] By this point, Franco was a mere bystander, incapacitated by advanced Parkinson's disease.

The new government initiated a harsh anti-terrorism law in mid-1975, which was essentially directed at any opposition of the regime. Two members of ETA in Burgos were sentenced to

[86] Paul Preston, *Franco: A Biography* (London: HarperCollins, 1993), p. 765.

death in August and September 1975, and another in Barcelona. Eight members of a separate organization, *Frente Revolucionario Antifascista y Patriota* ("Revolutionary Antifascist Patriotic Front"), received similar sentences through two more court martials.[87] The sentences were met by protests from governments and groups from around the world, including the Pope, but Franco rejected the pleas.

The court martials and the executions represented the death throes of the Franco regime. The government had in fact been shifting to a more reformist stance over the previous 15 years, and the sudden convulsion back to authoritarianism can also be read as a behind the scenes struggle for power, with the *Caudillo* clearly fading.

On October 15, 1975, Franco suffered a heart attack, and he died just over a month later, on November 20. He was buried, as he intended, in the Valley of the Fallen shrine, but the Franco era in Spain was over. Within three years, Spain would throw off the shackles of Francoism by drafting a new constitution and holding its first democratic elections since 1936.

The manner in which Franco's dictatorship was dismantled surprised many outside observers and was a tribute to decision-makers in Spain, especially when considering the bloodshed and violence of the 1930s. King Juan Carlos I took power in the aftermath of Franco's death and initially – as the *Caudillo* had hoped – seemed to offer continuity, leaving Carlos Arias as Prime Minister. Arias himself, thought relatively liberal by some, in fact wanted only minor changes to Franco's model.

However, another minister in Arias' government, Manuel Fraga, put forward a step-by-step reform program to full liberal democracy. Fraga had been a longstanding minister in Franco's administrations, albeit one with a reformist edge.[88] Adolfo Suárez also emerged as a pro-reform figure, and when Arias fell in 1976, Suárez was appointed Prime Minister. What emerged from this tumultuous period was an agreement to draft a new constitution and hold elections, which Suárez duly won in 1977. The regions were even granted considerable power under the new constitution, and by this time the Basque Country was experiencing unrest due to the rise of ETA, which would increase in the next decade.

Despite these changes, the pro-democracy reformers, as well as the new king, had to tread a fine line under pressure from Francoist conservatives and communists. In fact, after the fall of the right-wing Portuguese dictatorship in 1974, there was a fear among Western leaders that the entire Iberian Peninsula could adopt far-left governments.[89] These concerns, however, were to prove unfounded despite the successes of the more moderate center-left Spanish socialist party (PSOE) in the democratic era. The greater danger came from the right. In February 1981, a group of army officers, led by Antonio Tejero, stormed the Spanish parliament, taking the lawmakers

---

[87] Ibid, p. 775.
[88] Paul Preston, *Franco: A Biography* (London: HarperCollins, 1993), p. 728.
[89] Brendan Simms, *Europe: The Struggle for Supremacy 1453 to the Present*, (London: Penguin, 2014), p. 460.

hostage in an attempted coup. This coup, however, which took place 45 years after the rebellion that brought Franco to power, failed. King Juan Carlos appeared on Spanish television denouncing the plot, and it collapsed soon after. Tejero was imprisoned for 15 years.

Franco's Legacy

In some respects, Franco was a reluctant leader, but when he achieved power, he was highly reluctant to release the tight grip he had over Spanish society. The *Caudillo* was a wily, if unimaginative leader; the most he expected from the country was to return to the conservative, traditional and observant country which existed in his mind. Franco also wanted greater international clout for Spain, and that proved elusive throughout his lifetime.

By the time of his death in 1975, Franco held out some hope that the Spain he had forged in 36 years of rule would endure, but it was undone in short order. By the 1970s, many Spaniards wanted to be more like the rest of Europe, and following Franco's death, Spain converged politically with the rest of Europe remarkably easily.[90] Spain was admitted to the European Union in 1986, along with Portugal, partly as a reward for their respective transitions to democracy. Spain received substantial European funding, and as a result, its economy improved substantially. Despite some recent economic problems, today Spain is a rich country and has a high standard of living.

In many other respects, Franco's legacy has been eradicated. Spain is one of the most progressive and liberal countries in the world. Women gained equal legal rights after Franco's death, and in 2018, women hold a majority of posts in the Spanish Cabinet. Homosexuality and divorce have been legalized, and trade unions have been given greater influence. Even bullfighting has been outlawed in certain parts of Spain.

Franco held a particular animus towards Spain's regions, and his oppressive rule certainly bottled up resentment towards centralized rule. Although ETA eventually declared a ceasefire in their long campaign for Basque independence, separatism in Catalonia has only increased in recent years. Franco's desire to extinguish separatism essentially made it stronger than it was in 1936.[91] In late 2017, the Catalan parliament declared independence after a disputed referendum, but the Spanish government refused to recognize the results or negotiate with Barcelona. Catalan nationalists were keen to invoke the *Caudillo* during their recent campaign, with one describing the aftermath of the declaration and referendum as "a return to Francoism."[92]

---

[90] Nigel Townson, *Is Spain Different? A Comparative Look at the 19th and 20th Centuries* (Sussex Academic Press, 2015), p. 153.

[91] Paul Preston, *Franco: A Biography* (London: HarperCollins, 1993), p. 787.

[92] Michael Birnbaum, ' For some, Catalonia crackdown evokes memories of the dark days of Spain's dictatorship', *The Washington Post,* 9 November 2017, https://www.washingtonpost.com/world/europe/spanish-crackdown-on-catalonia-independence-effort-prompts-bitter-memories-of-franco-dictatorship/2017/11/08/b0ae6eac-bf14-11e7-9294-705f80164f6e_story.html?utm_term=.7634c70cb3e0, [accessed 25 June 2016]

One of the thorniest issues in post-Franco Spain was how to remember the dictator and his years in power, as well as the civil war's atrocities. Franco himself had remorselessly promoted his view of history, and Republicans and those who had fought on the Republican side during the civil war were demonized as alien, traitorous, and criminal. The political system he constructed over 36 years allowed no room for balance, no admission that the Nationalist side may have committed war crimes during the civil war, and no mention of the many human rights abuses of the Franco era. During his reign, Spain celebrated an annual "Day of Victory." However, while it may have been expected that the country would want to reinvestigate the crimes of the past and bring Franco's propaganda to light, this is not what happened. Ultimately, the new king and his group of reformers decided that debating the past would likely open old wounds and possibly stall attempts to progress into a democratic future.[93] A "Pact of Forgetting" was forged in the Spanish establishment and wider society, allowing the country to move on from its years of conflict and subsequent dictatorship. This was encapsulated in the 1977 Amnesty Law. As Paul Preston has noted, "During the transition to democracy, they (the Spanish) collectively displayed a political maturity which contradicted Franco's belief that they were incapable of living under a democratic system."[94] Spain was altered in a number of ways under the agreement, such as the repackaging of the Day of Victory to Armed Forces Day, but overall the Pact was maintained.

Nonetheless, many remain upset that the past was not confronted, arguing that only facing the truth would allow real reconciliation. In the 1990s, Judge Baltasar Garzón questioned the validity of the Pact, arguing that crimes against humanity had been committed and therefore must be confronted. Garzón's attempts were blocked by Spanish courts, but he did bring a case and an international arrest warrant on similar charges against Chilean dictator General Augusto Pinochet. Others have attempted to document unmarked mass graves from the civil war era, while many cities have changed Francoist street names and removed statues of the *Caudillo*.[95]

Francisco Franco's long life spanned from the last decade of the 19th century to the 1970s, and his view of Spain barely changed during his 82 years. Born into a conservative military family in the Atlantic province of Galicia, Franco was a nationalist who sought to end the perceived decline of Spain's international prestige, as well as a decay in its domestic values. Spain made a transition to democracy remarkably quickly after his death, but the cold, distant military man from Galicia had certainly left his mark on the country, and his influence is still being felt today.

Online Resources

Other books about Spain by Charles River Editors

[93] Omar G. Encarnación, 'Forgetting, in Order to Move On', *The New York Times*, 22 January 2014, https://www.nytimes.com/roomfordebate/2014/01/06/turning-away-from-painful-chapters/forgetting-in-order-to-move-on, [accessed 13 June 2018]

[94] Paul Preston, *Franco: A Biography* (London: HarperCollins, 1993), p. 786.

[95] Giles Tremlett, 'After Franco, the forgetting', *The Guardian*, 3 November 2007, https://www.theguardian.com/commentisfree/2007/nov/03/comment.spain, [accessed 26 June 2018]

Other books about Franco on Amazon

Further Reading

Victor Alba, *Transition in Spain: From Franco to Democracy* (New Brunswick: Transaction Books, translated by Barbara Lotito, 1978)

Michael Birnbaum, ' For some, Catalonia crackdown evokes memories of the dark days of Spain's dictatorship', *The Washington Post*, 9 November 2017, https://www.washingtonpost.com/world/europe/spanish-crackdown-on-catalonia-independence-effort-prompts-bitter-memories-of-franco-dictatorship/2017/11/08/b0ae6eac-bf14-11e7-9294-705f80164f6e_story.html?utm_term=.7634c70cb3e0

Tobias Buck, 'Facing up to Franco: Spain 40 years on', *Financial Times*, 8 May 2015, https://www.ft.com/content/5e4e6aac-f42f-11e4-99de-00144feab7de

Charles Bremner, 'Political extraditions are far from straightforward', *The Times*, 27 March 2018, https://www.thetimes.co.uk/article/political-extraditions-are-far-from-straightforward-hbfckxg60

Claude Canellas, Sonya Dowsett, Isla Binnie, 'Basque militants ETA surrender arms in end to decades of conflict', *Reuters*, 7 April 2017, https://www.reuters.com/article/us-spain-eta-idUSKBN1790YK

Omar G. Encarnación, 'Forgetting, in Order to Move On', *The New York Times*, 22 January 2014, https://www.nytimes.com/roomfordebate/2014/01/06/turning-away-from-painful-chapters/forgetting-in-order-to-move-on

Fiona Govan, 'Franco 'feared Hitler would kidnap him', *The Telegraph*, 28 November 2008, https://www.telegraph.co.uk/news/worldnews/europe/spain/3533400/Franco-feared-Hitler-would-kidnap-him.html

Chris Grocott, Review of 'Fear and Progress: Ordinary Lives in Franco's Spain, 1939-1975' by Antonio Cazorla Sánchez, *Reviews in History*, July 2010, http://www.history.ac.uk/reviews/review/936

George Hills, *Franco: The Man and His Nation* (London: Robert Hale, 1967)

The New York Times, 'Spain ends 13-year Gibraltar Blockade', 15 December 1982, https://www.nytimes.com/1982/12/15/world/spain-ends-13-year-gibraltar-blockade.html

Tatjana Pavlovic, *Despotic Bodies and Transgressive Bodies: Spanish Culture from Francisco Franco to Jesus Franco* (State University of New York Press, 2002)

Stanley G. Payne, *The Franco Regime, 1936–1975* (University of Wisconsin Press, 2011)

René Pélissier, 'Spain's Discreet Decolonization', *Foreign Affairs*, April 1965, https://www.foreignaffairs.com/articles/equatorial-guinea/1965-04-01/spains-discreet-decolonization,

Paul Preston, 'General Franco as a military leader,' *The transactions of the Royal Historical Society*, (4, 1994, pp. 21-41)

Paul Preston, *The Spanish Civil War: Reaction, Revolution & Revenge* (London: Harper Perennial, 2006)

Paul Preston, *Franco: A Biography* (London: HarperCollins, 1993)

Francisco J. Romero Salvadó, *20th-Century Spain: Politics and Society in Spain, 1898-1998* (Basingstoke: Macmillan, 1999)

Tim Reuter, 'Words Can Kill: Class Hatred And The Spanish Civil War', *Forbes*, 8 November 2013, https://www.forbes.com/sites/timreuter/2013/11/08/words-can-kill-class-hatred-and-the-spanish-civil-war/#3698d3312591

Paul Schue, 'Remember the Alcazar! The creation of nationalist myths in the Spanish Civil War: The writings of Robert Brasillach', *National Identities*, 10:2, November 2008, pp. 131-147.

Adrian Shubert, *A Social History of Modern Spain* (Taylor & Francis Group, 1990)

Brendan Simms, *Europe: The Struggle for Supremacy 1453 to the Present* (London: Penguin, 2014)

Herbert R. Southworth, *Conspiracy and the Spanish Civil War: The Brainwashing of Francisco Franco* (Routledge, 2002)

'M. Primo de Rivera: Coup and Success', *Spain: Then and Now*, http://www.spainthenandnow.com/spanish-history/m-primo-de-rivera-coup-and-success

Nigel Townson, *Is Spain Different? A Comparative Look at the 19th and 20th Centuries* (Sussex Academic Press, 2015)

Giles Tremlett, 'After Franco, the forgetting', *The Guardian*, 3 November 2007, https://www.theguardian.com/commentisfree/2007/nov/03/comment.spain

Free Books by Charles River Editors

We have brand new titles available for free most days of the week. To see which of our titles are currently free, click on this link.

Free Books by Charles River Editors

We have brand new titles available for free most days of the week. To see which of our titles are currently free, click on this link.

Discounted Books by Charles River Editors

We have titles at a discount price of just 99 cents everyday. To see which of our titles are currently 99 cents, click on this link.

CPSIA information can be obtained
at www.ICGtesting.com
Printed in the USA
BVHW041308181218
535877BV00019B/3300/P